AGGRESSIVE ENCOUNTERS

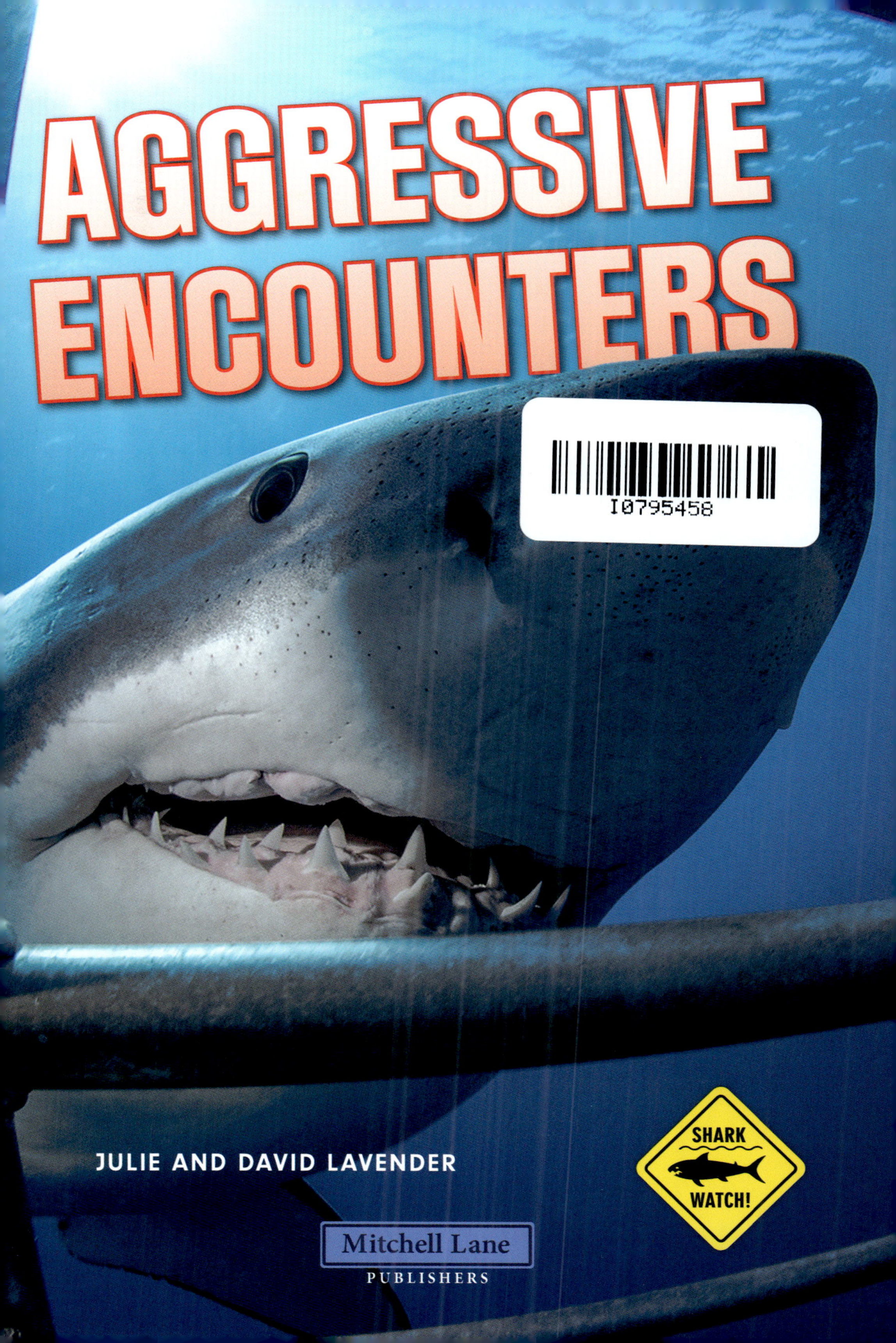

JULIE AND DAVID LAVENDER

Mitchell Lane
PUBLISHERS

Parent and Caregiver Tips for Creating Nonfiction Readers

The high-interest topics in the *Shark Watch!* series are sure to get your young reader excited about reading nonfiction. While exploring a fascinating subject, your reader will be introduced to new concepts, facts, ideas, and vocabulary.

Tips for Reading Nonfiction

Talk about Nonfiction

Explain that nonfiction books provide facts about real-world topics. When readers read nonfiction, they gain a rich understanding of the world. They build background knowledge that provides a foundation for learning and academic success.

Look at the Parts

This book contains the following helpful features. Share the purpose of each feature with your reader.

Photos, Captions, and Graphic Aids
The photos, captions, charts, maps, and other graphic aids in nonfiction texts contain a wealth of information. Help your reader identify different ways information can be displayed. A special feature, "A Closer Look," puts the spotlight on learning through images.

Sidebars
These extra tidbits of information help satisfy readers' curiosity and expand their knowledge.

Table of Contents
Located at the front of the book, this list shows the big ideas within the text and the page numbers where they can be found.

Glossary
Located at the back of the book, the glossary defines key words and phrases that are related to the topic. These words and phrases can be found in the text in colored or **bold** type.

Comprehension Questions (Fact Check)
Multiple-choice questions help readers self-check to make sure they understand what they read.

Index
Located at the back of the book, the index is an alphabetical list of topics and the page numbers where they can be found.

With a little help and guidance, your reader will be on their way to enjoying and learning from nonfiction books.

Mitchell Lane
PUBLISHERS

mitchelllanepub.com

2001 SW 31st Avenue
Hallandale, FL 33009

First Edition, 2026.
Authors: Julie and David Lavender
Designer: Rhea Magaro
Editor: Tricia Hoffman

Series: Shark Watch!
Title: Aggressive Encounters / by Julie and David Lavender
Hallandale, FL : Mitchell Lane Publishers, [2026]

Library bound ISBN: 979-8-89260-641-7
Paperback ISBN: 979-8-89260-653-0
eBook ISBN: 979-8-89260-651-6

PHOTO CREDITS
Alamy: Connect Images, 7; Cavan Images, 9, 29; Andrea Izzotti, 17; Nature Picture Library, 23, 29; Dreamstime: Tbarrat, 11; Izanbar, 14; Ondreicka, 24; iStock: atese, cover, 1; Shutterstock: Wallenrock, 8; sondem, 4; Kletr, 25; frantisekhojdysz, 20; karelnoppe, 27; wildestanimal, 15; Richard Whitcombe, 19; Vaclav Sebek, 28; StockStudio Aerials, 12; Foto-Foto-Foto-Foto, 5; VisionDive, 16, 28; Martin Prochazkacz, 22; Gustavo Miguel Fernandes, 21, 29; Ulrike Jordan, 10, 28; Ian Scott, 18;

CONTENTS

SHARK ENCOUNTERS

Aggressive encounters between sharks and humans are rare.

You've probably heard these facts: You are more likely to be struck by lightning than bitten by a shark. And there is a greater chance of being stung to death by bees than being eaten by a shark.

But still, you can't help but think about sharks when you take those first steps into the ocean. Will you see a **dorsal fin** headed your way?

TOOTHY TRUTHS

Most shark attacks occur within 35 feet (10 meters) of shore in water that is less than seven feet (two meters) deep.

What if you are that rare person who encounters, and is attacked by, a shark?

If you've ever been swimming off the coast of Florida or California, you've likely been up close to a shark and didn't know it. These encounters happen all the time. Sharks aren't usually hunting for humans, so they just swim right on by.

But on some occasions, something catches the shark's interest. Perhaps it sees that shiny bracelet you're wearing and decides to check it out. Then, it sees your feet wiggling, and it thinks they look like tasty fish. So, it opens its mouth, all those teeth flash, and ....

TOOTHY TRUTHS

In 2018, 13-year-old Keane Hayes survived a shark attack while lobster diving off the coast of southern California. He needed 1,000 stitches. He later returned to the water to swim, surf, and fish.

WHY DO SHARKS ATTACK?

No one knows exactly why some shark encounters turn aggressive. One theory is that sharks mistake humans for their normal prey. A surfer on a surfboard might look like a seal or sea turtle to the shark below. Or a diver in a black wetsuit may look like a sea lion underwater.

Another suggestion is that in the **murky** water of the **surf zone**, a shark confuses a human hand or foot with fish or other food. Or the shark may be defending its territory and thinks you're trespassing in its personal space.

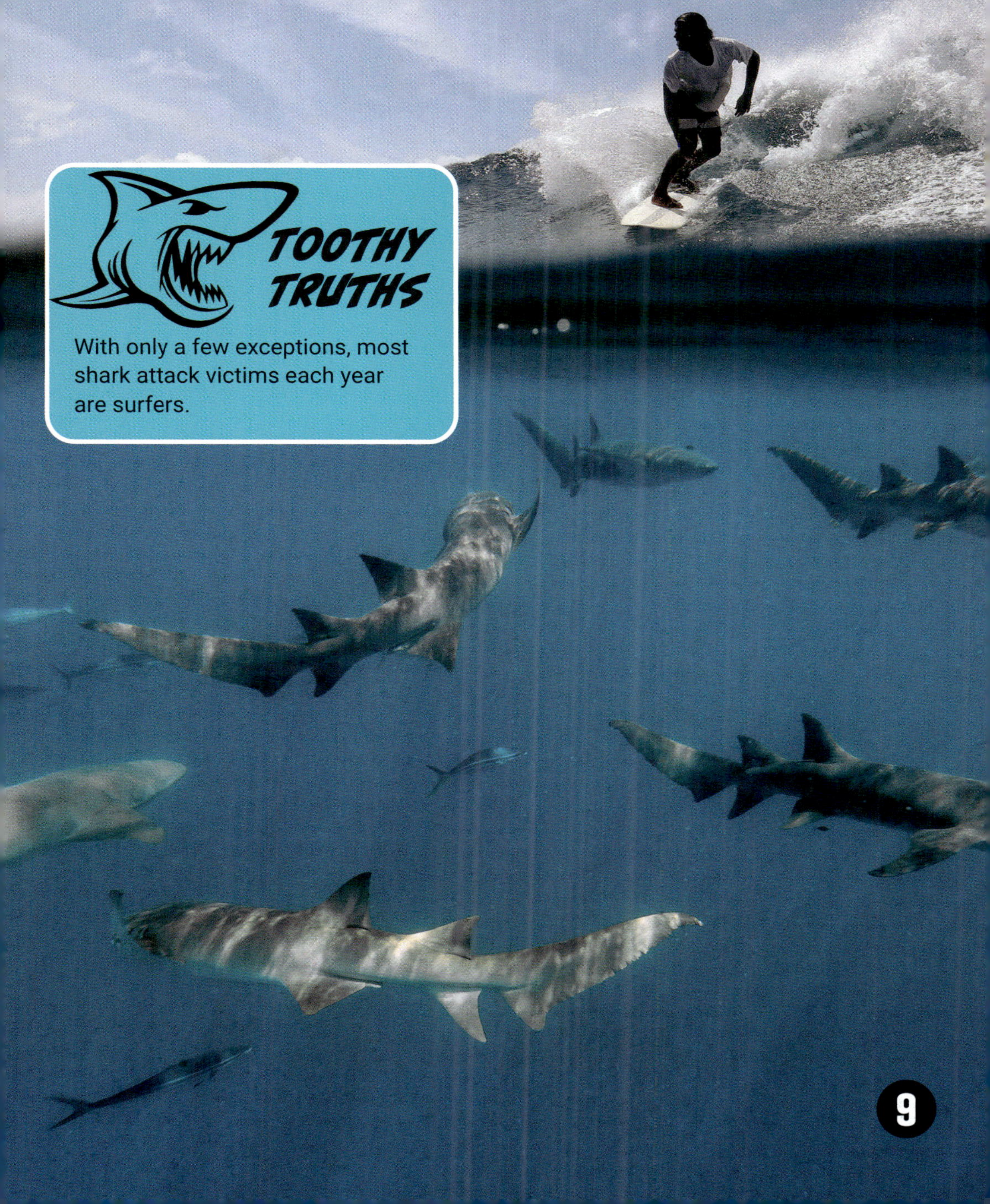

TOOTHY TRUTHS

With only a few exceptions, most shark attack victims each year are surfers.

HOW TO AVOID A SHARK ATTACK

Despite millions of people swimming and surfing in oceans every summer, shark attacks seldom happen—approximately 70 per year in the entire world. But you don't want to be one of the few that get bitten. Here's how to reduce the chances of that happening.

Choose a safe place to swim. Avoid beaches where there are seals or sea lions, or where there is sewage or garbage nearby. Stay away from deep water drop-offs like where a river empties into the ocean. Those are good places for a large shark to attack.

If you're in the water and see fish jumping, or notice schools of small fish swimming by, get out of the water. Small fish attract larger fish—the kind with lots of teeth!

Swim with a group. Sharks are more likely to pick out a lone swimmer. Also, if a shark does attack, someone can call for help.

Shiny jewelry glimmers like fish scales in water, so leave jewelry at home. Don't swim in the evening or at night, when more sharks are active and hunting.

If you have a fresh scrape or cut, stay out of the water. Sharks can smell blood in the water from up to a quarter mile (0.4 km) away!

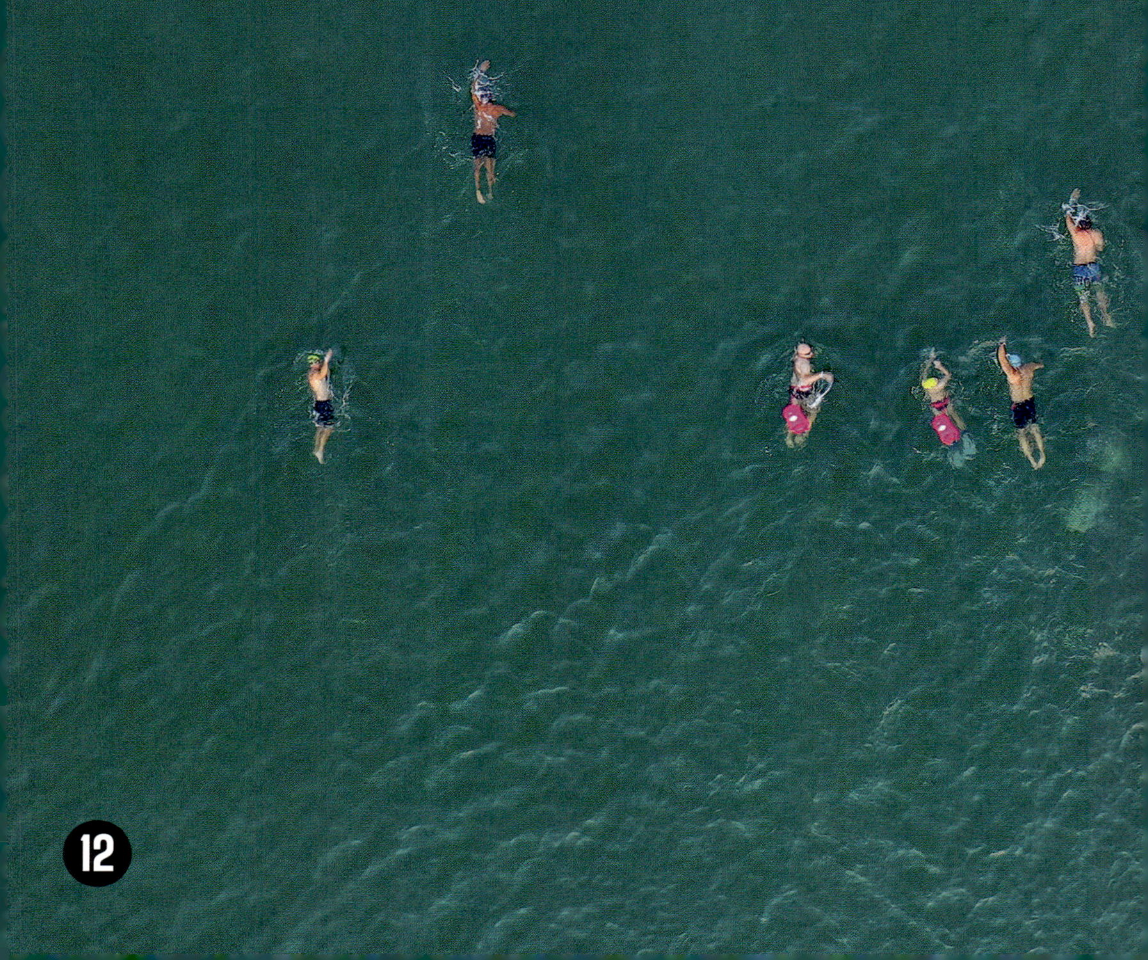

TOOTHY TRUTHS

Since 1975, the United States has had more shark attacks than any other country. Australia and South Africa are second and third on the list.

AGGRESSIVE BODY LANGUAGE

Sharks sometimes give warnings before they attack. The encounter first becomes aggressive when the shark shows **agonistic behavior**. It may perform certain actions when it is about to react aggressively, so be aware!

TOOTHY TRUTHS

Unfortunately, some victims received shark bites in what researchers call "provoked" attacks. They might have tried to feed a shark by hand, baited or **chummed** the shark in close, jabbed the shark with an object, or pulled the shark's tail.

Many sharks display threat **postures** as warning signs. They might arch their backs, hold their **pectoral fins** downward, point their snouts upward, or shake their heads.

An aggressive shark may also swim in a **figure-eight** pattern and open and close its mouth rapidly.

If you're snorkeling or swimming and see a shark acting like this, get out of the water. An attack is coming.

SO YOU'VE ENCOUNTERED A SHARK

What if you took all the precautions and still find yourself treading water with a shark circling you? What do you do now?

Do not turn your back on the shark. Keep turning to face it. Have a staring contest with the shark. Try to stay calm. Don't splash.

Back slowly toward the beach or boat. Make your movements slow, smooth, and steady.

If the shark moves closer, use anything you have, like a boogie board or face mask, to firmly push it away. Don't use your bare hands unless that's all you have.

If the shark's movements change from lazy circles to short charges before turning away at the last moment, you don't have much time. Get to a boat or the shore, fast! The shark is about to be in full attack mode. With a few swishes of its tail, it's coming straight at you.

There's not much you can do then. You can't outswim a shark. Prepare yourself. You are about to find out just how sharp those teeth are.

TOOTHY TRUTHS

Living with her family in Hawaii, Bethany Hamilton was 13 years old in 2003 when a shark bit off her arm and a large chunk of her surfboard. Bethany became an award-winning professional surfer. The movie ***Soul Surfer*** tells her shark attack story.

HOW TO SURVIVE A SHARK ATTACK

You can survive this. If the shark clamps down on your leg, fight back. Defend yourself any way you can. This is not a time to play dead.

In many attacks, the shark leaves after just one bite. The shark is looking for an easy meal. Don't be easy. Fight!

TOOTHY TRUTHS

Teen Addison Bethea, with help from her older brother, fought off a shark in Florida waters in 2022. Doctors removed her damaged leg below the knee. She hopes to become a physical therapist one day, so she can help people just like those who helped her.

Punch. Kick. Scratch. Claw. Hit the shark in the eyes and gills. Hitting the snout is good too, but it's close to the mouth. And the teeth.

Your efforts worked. The shark let go. You must act fast now. You're spilling a lot of blood in the water. The shark may come back. Or the blood may attract more sharks.

First, get out of the water. Next, apply pressure to the wound to stop the bleeding. And then, get help immediately.

BE PREPARED

Most sharks don't hunt humans. Sharks rarely become aggressive when they encounter people.

However, shark attacks do occur, and sometimes they are deadly. Follow common sense rules every time you enter the ocean. This reduces the chance of an aggressive encounter with one of these awesome beasts.

TOOTHY TRUTHS

Great white sharks are named for their white underbellies. But they are nicknamed "White Death" because they are responsible for more fatal attacks on people than any other shark species.

A CLOSER LOOK

Does the sign mean I can't swim at this beach? It doesn't say you can't swim ... but you shouldn't! If sharks have been sighted, stay on the beach. Don't risk swimming with sharks in the area.

If seals are swimming nearby, is it safe for me to swim here too? Unfortunately, no. These animals are cute and fun to watch, but they are also the favorite prey of many large sharks. The presence of seals or sea lions is a clue that you should NOT swim here.

How big can great white sharks get? Adult great white females can grow to more than 20 feet (6.1 meters) long. That's longer than three tall men laying down head-to-toe! A great white shark nicknamed "Deep Blue," seen near Hawaii, may be even bigger than that.

Why is the snorkeler poking this shark? The person is using a shark club to discourage and push away this curious shark. It may save his life!

Why are surfers involved in more shark attacks than anyone else? Surfers are often in deeper water than the average swimmer. And when a shark sees a surfer from below, a person with legs and arms dangling from a surfboard can be mistaken for a sea lion or sea turtle.

Did Bethany Hamilton ever surf again after the shark attack? Yes! Just one month after she lost her arm, the 13-year-old returned to surfing. Within two years, Bethany won her first national surfing title and became a professional surfer at the age of 17.

GLOSSARY

aggressive (uh-GRES-iv)
fierce or threatening

agonistic behavior (a-guh-NI-stik bi-HAYV-yur)
animal behavior relating to fighting, including aggression, defense, and avoidance

chummed (chuhmd)
dumping chopped or ground bait into the water to attract fish

dorsal fin (DOR-sl fin)
a flat, thin body part located on the backs of many fish and some marine mammals

figure eight (FIG-yur ayt)
moving or swimming in the shape of the numeral eight

murky (MUR-kee)
dirty, cloudy, or dark; difficult to see through clearly

pectoral fins (PEK-ter-uhl finz)
a pair of fins located behind a fish's head, one on each side

postures (PAHS-churz)
positions or stances of the body

surf zone (surf zohn)
the area of an ocean where waves break near the shoreline and create murky water

Fact Check

1. From below, a surfer may look like a _______.
   A. shark B. sea turtle C. octopus

2. To reduce the risk of shark attack, swim with a _______.
   A. group B. bat C. surfboard

3. In many shark attacks, the shark leaves after just one _______.
   A. minute B. scare C. bite

4. If a shark has you in its mouth, jab it in the _______.
   A. tail B. eye C. fin

Answers:
1. B, 2. A, 3. C, 4. B

Further Reading

BOOKS

Dubowski, Cathy East. *Shark Attack!* DK Publishing, 2015.

Hoena, Blake. *Shark Attack!: Bethany Hamilton's Story*. Bellwether Media, 2021.

Medina, Nico. *What Were the Shark Attacks of 1916?* Penguin Workshop, 2024.

ON THE INTERNET

How to Avoid Shark Attacks
www.floridamuseum.ufl.edu/discover-fish/sharks/how-to-avoid-shark-attacks
The Florida Museum site lists 13 tips for avoiding shark attacks.

Top tips on how to avoid a shark attack and what to do if you are attacked
www.bbc.com/news/newsbeat-33591730
With an included table of shark attacks since 1900, this article gives tips on how to avoid a shark attack and what to do if attacked.

Why Do Sharks Attack Humans?
www.americanoceans.org/facts/why-do-sharks-attack-humans
This article discusses possible reasons for shark attacks on humans, and includes a few tips on avoiding a shark attack.

INDEX

ABOUT THE AUTHORS

Authors Julie and David Lavender have experienced numerous shark encounters in the ocean, but none of the encounters ever turned aggressive. Julie and David are the parents of four adult children and grandparents of three little ones. Julie is a former teacher, and David served as a medical entomologist and wildlife biologist.